The Lost 90%

How to Invest in Your People and Grow Exponentially

Rob Marr

The Lost 90%

Independently Published

Copyright © 2022, Rob Marr

Published in the United States of America

210510-01873.2

ISBN: 9798425116383

No parts of this publication may be reproduced without correct attribution to the author of this book.

Here's What's Inside…

Foreword

When Rob asked me to write the foreword for his first book, I had to ask why? Many other people in his network have more recognizable names and careers than I do.

Rob's response was, "To me, it would be fitting that the person that helped me start my journey had a part to play in my first book. Without your intervention those few short years ago, there would be no book."

Well, when he said that to me, how could I refuse?

The Lost 90% is beyond powerful in its simplicity. This book should be on the "must-read" list for everyone in business who thinks training is the key to developing their people. In fact, according to Rob, if you change your spending on training and include the essential but often 'lost' elements of coaching and mentoring, you'll stop wasting money and help your people develop to their true potential. The results of boosting your spending will help your business grow exponentially.

Rob has a unique gift of turning complex topics into simple-to-understand methods. Once you see how he identifies more effective ways for you to grow your teams and business, you will be well on your way to finding your lost 90%!

Good luck. Stay safe. Be positive.

Nathan Gold

www.democoach.com

Introduction

Does this sound at all familiar?

There is a tired meeting room, a whiteboard, some lame group exercises, and some sandwiches getting stale in the corner; then someone speaks, so we nod along and try to sound engaged. We may even make some notes or ask the occasional question.

But - if we're honest - we're not present.

We're distracted. We check our emails during the breaks and sneak out to make 'urgent' calls. The minimal attention we had at the start fades as the day wears on. The few facts we've retained very rarely get used once we return to our usual routine. Six months later, we can barely recall what we learnt or even what the course was called.

If we're honest, this is what development looks like in most organisations: a tired format centred on PowerPoint, whiteboards, group exercises, and if we're really unlucky - some role play. The time, resources, and expense achieve very little. Unfortunately, this wasteful training has been the status quo for far too long.

This book is about a different methodology and an approach to people, which looks nothing like the dismal scene described above.

Instead of occasional training 'get-togethers', it is engaging and continuous.

Instead of one-way, it is collaborative.

Instead of hypothetical, it is real.

Instead of an obligation, it is an essential component of people's performance, growth, and job satisfaction.

It's based on a new ratio: 10% training, 20% mentoring, and 70% coaching. With a culture of mentoring and coaching markedly absent from most organisations, we call this 'The Lost 90%'.

This book will show you how to capture that Lost 90%, stop wasting money on training, help your people really develop, and see your business grow exponentially.

To Finding Your Lost 90%,

Rob

Chapter One
How We Teach Versus How We Learn

"For the things we have to learn before we can do them, we learn by doing them."
- Aristotle, Nicomachean Ethics (c. 334 BC - 330 BC)

Fundamentally, even though we may intuitively know how we learn best, the organisational structure and systems we encounter in life are often structured in the opposite way. As time passes, most organisations become overrun with outdated processes, tick-box development, and - most importantly - under-utilised people who fail to achieve their potential. The task has become the priority - the sole focus. That famous - albeit cliched - quote, 'Give a man a fish, and he'll eat for a day. Teach a man to fish, and he'll eat forever,' seems to count for nothing in the real world. We have become obsessed with 'the work'. The act of working. The value of working. But we have lost the value of learning almost completely.

This chapter title means a lot to me. All too often, I have unhappily observed how the way in which most organisations teach doesn't match the way in which people actually learn. Our experience and common sense have shown us countless times that the most useful way for us to attain a new skill, develop a new competence or build our confidence is through doing something rather than listening to someone, as opposed to being lectured or explained to.

The best way for us to learn is to get stuck in, get our hands dirty and develop expertise through repeated practice.

Think about an experience most of us have had - being taught to drive a car. We don't learn from the passenger seat: we learn from the driver's seat. My philosophy is as simple as that.

Yet - in most organisations - that very simple truth is rarely observed. As a result, I sincerely believe that something is fundamentally broken in organisations, that the training and development being provided is not fit for purpose. It doesn't correlate with how we learn, and even if training is delivered well, the follow-up is usually poor and, in many cases, non-existent. But whatever the delivery method, the simple fact remains - we learn best through personal actions, direct experiences, and immersive activities.

A Harvard study published September 4th, 2019, in the Proceedings of the National Academy of Sciences identified that although students felt as if they learned more through traditional lectures, they actually learned more when taking part in classrooms that employed so-called 'active-learning' strategies.

The lead author of the study, Louis Deslauriers, published a key study in Science in 2011 that showed just that. He knew that students would learn more from active learning, but many students and faculty remained hesitant to switch to it. He said. "a superstar lecturer can explain things in such a way as to make students feel like they are learning more than they actually are."

To illustrate this, Deslauriers and his co-authors designed an experiment that would expose students in an introductory physics class to both traditional lectures and active learning.

Over 15 weeks, two groups used identical class content where only active engagement with the material was manipulated

When the results were tallied, the authors found that students felt as if they learned more from the lectures but, in fact, scored higher on tests following the active learning sessions. "Actual learning and feeling of learning were strongly anti-correlated," Deslauriers said, "as shown through the robust statistical analysis by co-author Kelly Miller, who is an expert in educational statistics and active learning."

Those results, the study authors are quick to point out, shouldn't be interpreted as suggesting students dislike active learning. In fact, many studies have shown students quickly warm to the idea once they begin to see the results.

"In all the courses at Harvard that we've transformed to active learning," Deslauriers said, "the overall course evaluations went up."

Performance vs. perception

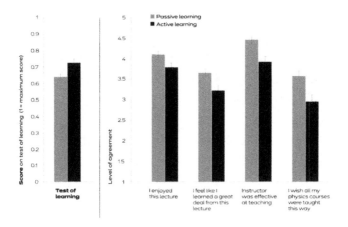

Source: "Measuring actual learning versus the feeling of learning in response to being actively engaged in the classroom," Louis Deslauriers, Logan S. McCarty, Kelly Miller, Kristina Callaghan, and Greg Kestin

Next Level Development Ratios

Having studied analysing professional growth throughout my career, I know that the percentages allocated to a people's development should roughly be:

10% Training - This should always be high quality, interactive and blended. There needs to be a single subject, short time frame, or multiple subject, medium time frame. There also needs to be positive stress for real learning to take place.

20% Mentoring - This should be consistent, immediate, and balance the constructive and useful with the honest and developmental.

70% Coaching - This should be aimed at challenging behaviours in both a positive and developmental way. Coaching should not be based on providing answers but on bringing accountability, responsibility, and ownership.

In my time working with organisations over the past 20 years, I've observed that there is - very frequently - a 'cliff edge'. If and when the training is delivered, the development often stops immediately after the training session or course. It's as if the delivery itself is sufficient and, therefore, a reasonable time for the training journey to legitimately end.

In short, 90% of the development people need to grow, thrive and add value, is either lost or simply not present in the first place. If this was true for any other resource that businesses utilised to achieve their objectives, it would obviously be addressed as a matter of strategic urgency.

Example: The Typical Onboarding Process: Sink or Swim

Let's look at a new joiner being 'onboarded' into an organisation. Often, the first few weeks are focused on upskilling and training for their new job, and many times, if not always, they're told how to do it. This typically entails someone sitting next to them, detailing a particular process or system, usually by telling them, not by getting them truly engaged.

There may be some element where they have a little practice, but because there's often so much information to pass over and so little time to do so, managers tend to shortcut and simply 'tell' people the required information. A few weeks later, the onboarding simply stops. Sometimes the new recruit might get a mentor or a buddy, but more often, they don't.

So, after those first sessions, it's usually up to that person to sink or swim.

In many organisations, new joiners have a six-month period of 'probation' after which they're evaluated, and it's decided whether they're going to keep their job or not. The organisation does not have any strong evidence to suggest why they should or shouldn't stay, other than the opinions of the leader or the line manager on whether they're doing a good job. Even though, contradictorily, they haven't equipped the new employee to do the job well with a 100% development process. We advertise a job based on the human traits needed and then manage them on the tasks. Where is the individual in any of this? Is it any wonder that people leave or feel disenfranchised?

I have often seen how the onboarding team does little to help if the culture in the organisation isn't centred around people. They will be sharing all the 'hacks' on what it takes to survive rather than thrive.

Issues & Themes from the example:

- Multiple subjects but short time frames
- Focused on giving the person the tasks
- Little follow-up or support in most cases after the onboarding is complete

- Focus on saving time and speed rather than long term success of the person
- The priority is the work being done, not the development of a new person to the organisation

Learning How to Learn - The Right Environment

Before we talk about learning steps, I think it's important to recognise that people don't always view learning as a positive activity.

Everyone has a different experience of learning. There are a number of factors that influence how positively people are disposed towards learning. In one of my favourite books 'Mindset', Dr. Carol Dweck argues powerfully on adopting a Growth Mindset versus a Fixed Mindset. The attitudes we take towards learning will obviously have a huge impact on how easy we are to teach!

I think we all have different attitudes towards learning, usually based on how we were taught when younger. However, it isn't just the initial learning that is the main issue - it's how we support that learning journey. We all go through the same steps to learn any skill or learn any particular task, but the environment in which we are learning has a fundamental impact on how effective we are at it.

If employees in your organisation aren't positively inclined towards learning, how positively inclined can the organisation be? We don't just have the challenge of engaging people in a positive learning journey but also face the challenge of putting aside any prejudices they hold from the past.

Is the Cost of the Lost 90%?

The cost of not understanding the learning and development people need is high. A typical organisation usually has:

- Average morale
- Inconsistent motivation
- Poor engagement
- Significant staff turnover
- Silos
- Task orientation
- People only taking responsibility for their jobs

- No real sense of purpose but instead a 'Living for the weekend' attitude.

The work or the tasks become the thing, and it's something to get through by 5 pm on Friday rather than to learn from and grow.

The cost is not just a lack of productivity, innovation, or creativity. There is also the very real and measurable cost of high staff turnover, lack of engagement, and the ensuing poor performance. If you were to consider your organisation right now, how many people could you honestly say are genuinely fulfilling their potential? Think about the gap between that reality and where the organisation could be. Imagine if people were doing everything they could, rather than that which they are 'allowed' or confined to do.

Imagine if we actually invested in The Lost 90% as a source of competitive advantage?

Sadly, for many organisations, it seems to be a never-ending cycle of people in, people out without their true capabilities ever being drawn out.

This amazing resource remains sadly under-utilised, even though our people are the most expensive resource that we have. Ironically the process of recruiting and 'training' new employees is itself hugely cost-intensive, only for them - all too frequently - to depart soon afterwards.

In addition, of course, the intangible cost is equally important in terms of company morale and culture.

The potential in your organisation is your people.

Typical Training = Necessary Evil

The classic situation that I see in organisations is that training is often perceived as a tick-box exercise - a 'necessary evil'. It's something that has to be done because it has to be done. There are different reasons for this depressing state of affairs: training is used to correct poor performance, is functional in terms of the specific work required, or is simply considered to be a mandatory obligation.

A true understanding of how we develop people in most organisations is surprisingly poor. When such a valuable investment is minimised, put aside, deprioritised, or cut short, it really sends a terrible message to our people. Training can be a hugely valuable investment as the beginning of a learning journey.

Unfortunately, it can be viewed as expensive in terms of time, energy, and lost hours on the job when the work is our focus. However, I can't think of any area in life where we receive a service or product that we wouldn't want the person providing that service to be well trained! How can one of the very things that help us improve, innovate and perform better be seen as a nuisance or distraction? It is because we have lost the value of people. We are preoccupied with work, tasks, and productivity and fail to see the more substantive benefits in true development.

Task-Focused Training vs. People-Focused Training

Think about how a leader is tasked with developing their team; that person is learning within that process. If the focus is on the task, then the focus can never be on the person. The teaching becomes focused on the value of the task to the company and not making a mistake. With this misalignment, the learning becomes focused on how that individual delivers the task to minimise risk and ensure compliance to a pre-established system.

We miss out on the most important element: the person in receipt of the training that has almost unlimited capacity to make things better.

It's nearly every story in every business or organisation in every situation. The challenge is always set as a relentless execution of tasks, targets, and delivering on KPIs. A token amount of energy is put into how we teach people and how they learn.

We can and should create a powerful dynamic environment to teach and learn together to grow and develop the organisation. The rewards can be exponential for BOTH the people and the organisation.

A Practical Tip

In the next chapter of the book, we will discuss identifying what type of organisation you are in. A good tip is to start with a self-assessment or a self-analysis of your organisation's approach towards learning development and your people. You can fill out our quick diagnostic here at https://www.yourlearninglegacy.com/business-diagnostic

www.yourlearninglegacy.com/business-diagnostic

We've categorised the organisational types in the next chapter. There are four very specific types that I've identified. One of the ways that you can improve is by recognising where you are initially, so you can start to move towards the organisation you wish to be.

Chapter Two
The Four Types of Organisations

"Even though worker capacity and motivation are destroyed when leaders choose power over productivity, it appears that bosses would rather be in control than have the organization work well."
- Margaret J. Wheatley, How is Your Leadership Changing? 2005

There's one thing that most people would agree with - organisations that meaningfully invest in their people outperform organisations that don't. When an organisation's focus is just aligned to shareholder interest (which frequently equates to the return of short-term value to those shareholders), performance is limited. This is because the primary focus will solely be on tasks, efficiency, cost reduction, and 'sweating the human asset' to produce the highest output possible for the least amount of money.

Job contracts are increasingly likely to be split between a basic wage plus an incentivised earning 'opportunity.' Sometimes, half the salary of an employee can be based on bonuses. This is fine, of course, if the market is driving the performance of the organisation upwards but quickly changes when it dips. It is always the people that are first to go. It is depressing how many businesses float or sink in the constantly fluctuating bull or bear markets. The leaders take the credit when the market is strong, and the employees take the blame when it isn't.

Too often, organisations are focused on the result that we want rather than how we will achieve that result. No one would think running a Marathon was possible if all we did was talk about the result. It is the training, mentoring, and coaching that deliver the result. The training football players do during the week delivers the results on the weekend. One of the key aspects of an athlete being considered elite is how hard they train. Why isn't that the measure in organisations? Why do we laud people for learning and improving in sport but not in business?

We know if we focus on skills development, then the results will follow. If you think about how an athlete trains, the result is the hitting of their targets in their respective disciplines. However, the countless hours, days, weeks, and months spent training and being coached and supported clearly underpins their success. If they just focused on the event and went from event to event without learning, improving, or changing, they would never become 'elite'.

Your organisation has the opportunity to change. You have the opportunity to focus on how results are delivered; not just the end result itself.

Taking Time to Learn

If, for example, an organisation has a significant sales problem but the learning and development time dedicated to upskilling the team to increase sales is minimal, then it can be pretty much guaranteed the result won't be what is desired. We talk about the importance of the result but never stop the activity long enough to really understand what is needed, who we can learn from, what is working well, and what isn't.

We know that people need time to learn, develop, and enhance their skills through lots of repetition, but we tend to focus on the outcome alone. The training cost is often seen as too high, even if the cost of missing the target can be far higher.

It is worth noting the quality of a lot of training is surely to blame here as well. Never mind the complete lack of mentoring and coaching. If, as outlined in my introduction, the experience is a mind-numbing 'snore-fest', then no wonder it is so easily ignored!

"Students learn what they care about and remember what they understand" - Ericksen 1984, p. 51.

In Summary

As they often say in sport, if you focus on the performance, the results will follow. In business, we only seem to focus on the results.

There are four types of organisations I have identified, so I'll start with what I would classify as the most demotivating or most demoralising type to work.

1. Task-Focused Organisation

Essentially, this tends to be a top-down culture, where the leaders decide what the strategy is and tell everyone else what to do. The culture and people are task-oriented, focused on executing a particular element of that strategy; no more, no less. The morale tends to be very low. The enthusiasm tends to be low. Creativity is poor. Engagement is weak, as are idea sharing, collaboration, teamwork. There are very seldom true values present, and even if they are, they are tokenistic in nature.

There's no meaningful investment in training, mentoring, or coaching. People are expected to do their jobs. They're a literal human resource. The requirement is that they come in on time, work hard, leave, and get paid, and that's the end of their development. That's type number one.

2. Reactive Organisation

The second type of organisation that I frequently see is Reactive, where the focus is on the business needs only. There is training, mentoring, and coaching, but it's usually mandatory or used to correct poor performance.

For example, it might be that sales are down, so sales training is required. It could be that mystery shopper scores are poor, and training is provided. It could be food hygiene, but the training is only required because the law requires them to provide it. There are no personal development plans. No one has a career path. If they do, it's self-authored. It's not created or defined by the company. It is something that exists in the individual rather than in the organisation.

Training, mentoring, and coaching are usually based almost entirely on external factors. What's happening to the business or is required of the business creates a need for training. It is not because there's a desire to develop people. Training is viewed as a cost that rarely delivers a return on investment and is deemed 'a necessary evil'.

3. Process-Driven Organisation

The third business is what I call a Process-Driven organisation, which is usually driven by the HR function. The training exists. There is a very clearly documented approach to the development of people, but it's very much standardised, off-the-shelf, and frequently in-house. There's zero personalisation; it's pretty much ticking the boxes. It's often subsidised and supported by a third party.

The aim is not to get the best training. The aim is to get the most cost-effective training. Boxes are ticked, and people are appraised, even though the quality of the appraisal is frequently poor, uninspiring, and often pretty demoralising. The manager or the leader doesn't have much skill or interest to do the appraisal well and has often pre-filled the forms or documents that the employee has to agree with.

There's very little mentoring and coaching in process-driven organisations. The way they develop people is by training them. As we have established, the chances of a real transfer of knowledge and confidence and competence building don't happen through standard training alone.

There are some larger Process-Driven Organisations that have excellent L & D functions where they have robust processes established to create, deliver and check the implementation and ROI of all the development work. But as a percentage - sadly - these are the exception rather than the rule. Often due to time constraints, budgetary pressure, or shifting focus, these L & D teams can be driven to work in a way that they haven't bought into or aren't suited to.

The model most often used in my experience is the Fitzpatrick Model, which is extremely robust. It has 4 stages of evaluation:

1. Reaction
2. Learning
3. Behaviour
4. Result

Sometimes the organisation may have a 5th stage for Return On Investment.

Where I see the flaw is that the management of these processes is the responsibility of the L & D department rather than the managers and leaders on the ground. Unless the whole organisation is brought into the development of its people, they can often be just accommodated rather than embraced.

4. Hybrid Organisation

The Hybrid Organisation is a mix of any of the other three types of organisations. The types can, of course, vary by department, division, location, or any other variable you could mention that exists in any organisation. I have seen many times that the leader sets the tone. The more indifferent an organisation is towards having people as the centre of their focus, the more likely it is that the organisation will be Hybrid. It is dictated in the micro rather than the macro.

Hybrid Organisations are the most common in my experience. They are living proof of the overall attitude that exists - the organisation might as well be saying - 'people aren't worth focusing on, so we'll just let the organisation find its own level'.

Another Way

There is, of course, another way to go where you create a Learning Legacy Organisation, delivering Exponential Growth through its people. The process to achieve that is detailed in my book 'Your Learning Legacy,' and more details can be found at our website www.yourlearninglegacy.com

Learning Legacy Organisation (Next Level)

So what does a Learning Legacy Organisation have in place that enables Exponential Growth?

Firstly, learning is the priority, not the organisation's task. There is accountability, ownership, and responsibility throughout. There is a culture of leaders and learners, where all training intends to turn the trainers into teachers. The fundamental goal of teaching someone how to do something is that they, at some point, become a teacher themselves.

Teaching How to Teach

By teaching people how to teach, and by encouraging and then creating an environment in which they can teach others, the organisation can achieve a rapid level of growth that can't be achieved in the other four types of organisation that we've just briefly looked at. The entire focus is on growth, not tasks.

Even when mistakes are made, they're used as opportunities to learn, grow, develop and accelerate the business. They're not viewed as opportunities to criticise, critique, or performance-manage people. The entire focus is on how we, collectively as a group of people, achieve the goals. There are high levels of communication, engagement, consistent teamwork, positivity towards learning and development opportunities, a strong focus on internal development rather than external recruitment, and powerful opportunities for the business and the employees to be successful as the organisation grows.

Chapter Three
Focusing on the Eight Stages of Learning or Change

"Deep learning is hard work. The effort involved in active learning can be misinterpreted as a sign of poor learning."
- **Louis Deslauriers**

When we talk about learning, really what we are talking about is change. Adapting a new set of skills, attitudes, and behaviours to be able to improve our competence at something; or learn something new. Ultimately we are learning to change.

Before change can happen, it is, of course, important to know what type of organisation you are in. We covered this earlier, but I'd like you to think about the answer to that question now with a little more nuance.

In her article on the 'Psychology Today' website Amy C. Edmondson, Ph.D., talks about Psychological Safety. There are some useful signposts here to take note of. Amy observes 3 distinct organisational stages:

1. **Toxic Unsafe Environment** - We hold back from voicing concerns; we engage in 'backstabbing', we focus much of our energy on self-protection, and we fear that what we say will be used against us in the near future

2. **Stable Environment** - We hold back ideas and perspectives to appear competent, reliable, and trustworthy. Cross competence conversations feel like debates or negotiations, and we get little payoff for our agile initiatives

3. **Strategic Environment** - We collaborate effectively across silos and expertise; consistently speak up with ideas, questions and problems; effectively engage in exploratory dialogue on high importance topics; engage in conflict without fear of reprisals and respond effectively to change in our environment

I love these definitions from Dr. Edmondson as they so clearly outline the risks we face from a poor culture in accessing engagement in any learning process. **For any seed to grow, the ground has to be fertile**.

Assuming the environment in the organisation is ready for learning or change, let us look at the stages needed to successfully build a skill, attitude, or behaviour. I'll break this down into three parts - before, during, and after.

Before

I have based this part of the process on the work done by James Prochaska and Carlo DiClemente in their 'Stages of Change'.

1. Pre-Assessment
2. Assessment
3. Planning

During

For stages 4-7, I am using Martin Broadwell's '4 Levels of Teaching' as the base.

4. Unconscious incompetence
5. Conscious incompetence
6. Conscious competence
7. Unconscious competence

After

8. Teach Others

Those eight stages correlate to how all of us as human beings learn, from driving a car to making a cup of coffee to performing a complex operation in an operating theatre. We all have to go through the stages of learning.

It is important to recognise that learning a skill and learning attitudes or behaviours are no different as far as the brain is concerned.

Defining the Stages of Learning

Before:

Pre-Assessment

Organisationally, this is interesting. Pre-assessment is where there is a lack of awareness or understanding that there may be a problem or something new to learn. The behaviours are ingrained. The culture is set. The die is cast.

That is not to say the people within the organisation don't know that change is needed - not at all. In fact, the signs will be well and truly there. Some obvious, and some less so. The obvious signs can include high staff turnover, lack of cooperation internally, customer complaints, and high sickness or absenteeism. The less obvious signs are overall performance, inconsistency of results, lack of interest or encouragement in or for internal promotions. The less obvious signs are easily blamed on external factors. There can be a tendency to blame the people in the organisation for not handling the external issues well. This stage needs someone with enough authority to speak up. To challenge the status quo. This is why organisations remain stuck.

People understandably don't want to put their hands up because of the possible consequences.

Assessment

This stage is when there are enough voices to raise the idea that change may be needed. There is consensus at meetings; there is excitement building amongst some people or entire teams, there is a genuine belief things are going to possibly go in a new and positive direction. You find people sharing their views and others enthusiastically agreeing. On a personal learning journey, we get lots of encouragement from our friends and colleagues - we listen to them and, more importantly, we listen to ourselves.

You see that change may be possible, but you are not sure how to start. This can be a stage when outside help is sought. Expertise is brought to the table, and suggestions are made for what could be possible.

This is obviously another big risk phase because of the cost. Cost is usually the biggest threat to change: a focus solely on the bottom line. Ideally, the focus would be on the return on investment possible, but many organisations don't see it that way.

Organisations and people can still view the challenges as not being that serious, especially if they feel they are performing or doing 'fine'. All too often, this kind of business will wait for the problems to hit before they invest in a solution. They wait for the symptoms to present before they address the underlying cause of the problem. Often at this stage, change can come too late, and the goodwill or enthusiasm that was there to change or learn can evaporate quickly if it is left too long.

Planning

This is a very exciting part of the change and learning journey. This is when what we thought was possible turns into a strategy and tactics. It is when consensus has been reached by ourselves or by the organisation that we are in. We want to change and learn, and it is time to plan. It is important at this stage to ensure that several elements are in place and aligned:

- We have the right support and accountability to make sure we follow through

- We have measures of what success can be
- We agree on those measures with the people supporting the journey
- We remain flexible - <u>not hitting early milestones need not invalidate the plan</u>
- We focus on the benefits to change and learning, not the cost
- We agree to celebrate successes of all sizes along the way

The plan needs to be shared with everyone! People can't support what they don't know or understand. I encourage people to write their plans in pencil, not pen. We have to be allowed to adapt and flex whilst learning, changing, and growing.

During:

Unconscious incompetence

Unconscious incompetence is that wonderful stage of learning when we don't know how bad we are at something, but we're happy to give something a go. We are open to change, and we have an opportunity to develop in front of us.

This stage can sometimes be forced upon people in some organisations, and that is often unhealthy. This is where some people may be sent to training to 'fix performance', for example.

This stage is often brief in my experience. It doesn't take long once we begin to learn something new for the challenge to be felt by the learner. Again our attitudes can have a huge impact on how successful we are at progressing to the next stage. This is when our support people and groups are hugely important, as well as accountability from others.

Conscious Incompetence

Once we begin learning, we rapidly move to conscious incompetence. **This is a strong risk area**. Conscious incompetence is when we become aware of how bad we are at what we're trying to learn.

This stage is important in learning because most people quit what they're trying to learn. This is where most people give up learning to drive. This is where most people quit giving up smoking. It's where most people abandon a new diet or discipline. We become conscious of how incompetent we are at the new thing. It's not an ingrained natural behaviour. It's new, it's frightening, it's different. It's not like what we're used to. In many ways, this is what makes changing organisations and people so fundamentally difficult.

For years, they've been invested over and over and over again in doing something a particular way. To do something different is hard, not because it's hard, but because we haven't been through the stages of learning. Conscious Incompetence is a very risky stage from an organisational point of view.

It's where most people give up on implementing the new training they've been provided with.

Ebbinghaus has called this the forgetting rule, where we forget 80% of what we've learned within 48 hours of learning it. If there's no accountability to the learning, we often drift away very quickly after we've learned it.

Conscious Competence

On the assumption that we do continue - which can be a big assumption - we advance to conscious competence. This is where we can actively do the thing we're trying to do, but we're not yet fluid or fluent at it. We have seen the evidence for feeling positive, but we have not reached the whole group or hit our own personal milestones. We can do this, but.....

We're not masterful yet.

This is the point when you are competent enough to pass a set of rigorous criteria in terms of your ability - you are competent. We hear of positive changes that are happening and seeing some good results. But we are not there yet.

This stage represents another great risk factor; this is another area where people quit. Because we're not masterful yet, we can have one incident because we're not unconsciously competent. It tends to be derailed by a problem or a crisis.

For a personal example, if you are driving your car, you've started driving, you're not that confident, but you can do it, and then you have a near-miss or a minor 'prang'. For many people, that's the reason to stop driving.

It's not a very strong stage of learning, conscious competence.

We can do it, but it's not behavioural yet. It's risky, and it's often a point of slipping back where you can see some good early results. Most organisations can point to good early results post-training, particularly those with a learning focus.

But it often fades away through a lack of mentoring or coaching because the learning has not been reinforced or something challenging happened. The person gave up on the new skill.

Unconscious Competence

This is where we become unconsciously competent. We can do it without conscious thinking.

Once we become unconsciously competent, we become really good at what we hope to change or learn without much effort. This is the stage when change has happened - the learning has been acquired - we are on a new path. This is where real innovation and rapid growth can happen. This is the stage at which confidence can be built to start new challenges and change and grow. We have learned how to be different. We have broken away from the old and into the new. We feel good about ourselves, and the organisation feels good about what it sees in its results.

This stage is a stage when we need to double down on our investment and our efforts. Now that we are going, we need to keep going. Processes need to be built to support the continuation of growth.

Here is the key point to focus on:

At this stage, the objective is simple - just don't stop. This is just the beginning. We have learnt how to learn - we need to leverage this at every point in our lives and at every part of the organisation.

After:

Teach Others

This is, for me, the most satisfying part of the journey of learning - the process of change.

We get to teach others what we learn. We get to give back and help others along. We get to ripple our growth throughout our teams, our friends and family, and our colleagues. A rising tide lifts all boats - we don't rise on our own but with others. We get to share the experience. We get to be part of something.

Sharing your knowledge feels good. Sharing what you know feels good. It creates a ripple effect as people then want to give back to you. This stage is when people really and truly are at the centre of an organisation. The work, the tasks become secondary. The purpose is to learn and grow from every piece of work, and through that, we hit the objectives we set for ourselves and for the organisation.

Your Brain Doesn't Differentiate

It's important to highlight that your brain doesn't differentiate between good skills and bad skills. Good change and bad change. It just trusts the process.

For example, someone with a bad diet can be good at having a bad diet. They can be unconsciously competent at feeding themselves poorly through repetition. It's not that they want to be good at it on a logical level. However, on a human level, they exercised that muscle so strongly it's become their natural innate behaviour, and to learn how to do something different involves a substantial behaviour change.

It's the most comfortable place people can be. It's not anything they even think about. It's part of who they are at that point.

Once you develop any skill in something, it goes beyond the scale and turns into your identity. It becomes who you are. Initially, it becomes a role you play; then, it becomes who you are. We become very attached to who we are, even if it logically doesn't make sense or objectively we don't respect that persona. If you continue with the analogy of someone with a bad diet, they often actively make jokes about how bad their diet is, even though that could be life-threatening for them in the long term.

In February 2018, The New York Times reported the impressive results of a new study showing that "diet quality, not quantity" was the key to weight loss. Focusing on eating plenty of vegetables and unprocessed foods was a better strategy than counting calories, according to the JAMA study, in which more than 600 people adopted one of two healthy diets for a year. Near the end of the article, however, was a strange caveat: People in both groups had consumed fewer calories than they normally would have. Suddenly, the article's claims about quality versus quantity seemed suspect.

On reading the article, the author realised the takeaway from the study was not about diets; it was about teaching.

After all, the basic science of nutrition hasn't changed: People who consume more calories than they burn tend to gain weight. But just telling people to cut down on calories isn't enough to change their behaviour.

What did the researchers behind the JAMA study do differently? They taught people how to adopt the sort of eating habits that naturally lead them to consume fewer calories.

Overview

Are People Disposed to Learn?

Before any learning can take place, the learner must be well-disposed towards the idea of learning. One of the challenges that many people have is a fixed mindset towards learning and development. They think it's not about growth but about talent. Rather than being open to learning new things, they're actively resistant to them. Rather than viewing learning as an opportunity for them to grow, they view it as a threat or an indication of a lack of competence on their behalf. They view it as a negative criticism rather than a positive opportunity. If someone is actively engaged against it, it's very hard to teach that person anything.

The longer people have been in a system or organisation (of the type that was detailed earlier in the book), the more likely they are to be entrenched against learning new things.

One of the Biggest Challenges You'll Face

One of the biggest challenges I face as a trainer when I start any program with any organisation is how low the expectations are. That's because they've not been engaged in the process before the training. No one has ever asked for their opinion.

If they've been told that their performance isn't up to scratch, they traipse into the training room, virtual or actual. Most people have pretty low expectations. One of the most frequent comments I get on my feedback forms is, 'That was way better than I expected.' People are not entering most training environments expecting the experience to be a positive one.

They're thinking about it as 'This is tiresome, it's going to be boring. This guy is going to be rambling on for hours, and I know all of this stuff already. I did a similar training program three years ago on this…'

People often have fixed mindsets. They have a fixed idea about what learning is and what training can be. The standard is so fundamentally poor anywhere in the world that you go that by the time people get into the training room, they're already completely ill-disposed towards the idea of learning anything because they think you're the enemy.

How to Intentionally Improve

The organisation's culture, as we have detailed, is usually the problem in the first place because the focus is on tasks. People are always thinking about what they should be doing instead of the training.

If you attend a one-day training course on customer service, to use a generic example, you are not thinking about your development. You're thinking, 'I have so much work to do. I don't have time to go on this training course!' Rather than thinking about the value of your long-term, ongoing development, you're thinking about how much work you have to do.

At that point, you have to go back to the organisation that is clearly focused on the tasks, not the person.

You don't have people engaged with learning, because organisations are not engaged with learning.

One of the most powerful steps an organisation can take (and it sounds incredibly simple) is being 100% clear on the difference between the tools of training, mentoring, and coaching. Most organisations don't know what the difference is, and they don't know how or when to use them. Therefore, they either don't use them at all or frequently use them poorly.

We are going to detail these vital yet different tools next. You will then better understand what exact situation you are faced with and what is the appropriate action to take.

Key Questions:

Is this a training problem?

Is this a mentoring problem?

Is this a coaching problem?

Rather than trying to solve a coaching problem with a training solution, you can solve a training problem with a training solution, a coaching problem with a coaching solution, and so on and so forth.

The Importance of Everyone Buying into the Process

When it comes to changing mindsets, it's important to get the buy-in from everyone who needs to be involved first. It can feel as significant as changing who they see themselves to be. This is not easy.

This is why, from an organisational point of view - and this goes back to our first chapter - it makes so little sense that training is used in a narrow way because it doesn't address how we are.

We are environmental in the way that we change. We have to see change around us to make change easy for ourselves. Let's go back to that example of someone with a bad diet. They start eating more healthily, having more balance, more structure, small meals five times a day, all of that good stuff, but everyone else in the house is ordering a pizza every evening. It's very hard for that person to change behaviour, not because they're weak, but because everyone else is weak.

What happens to growth-oriented individuals in a negative environment? They leave.

Treating Your Best People... The Worst

Simon Sinek tells a great story about how it feels when you treat your best people the worst, how it can look, and the response you get from your best people when you treat them the best.

'A few months ago, I stayed at the Four Seasons in Las Vegas. It is a wonderful hotel. The reason it's a wonderful hotel is not the fancy beds. Any hotel can go and buy a fancy bed. The reason it's a wonderful hotel is the people who work there. If you walk past somebody at the Four Seasons and they say hello to you, you get the feeling that they wanted to say hello to you. It's not that somebody told them that they say hello to all the customers and say hello to all the guests. You feel that they care.

Now, in their lobby, they have a coffee stand. One afternoon, I went to buy a cup of coffee, and there was a barista by the name of Noah who was serving me. Noah was fantastic. He was friendly and fun, and he was engaging with me. I had so much fun buying a cup of coffee. I think I gave a 100% tip. He was wonderful.

As is my nature, I asked Noah, 'Do you like your job?' Without skipping a beat, Noah says, 'I love my job!' I followed up, and I said, 'What is it that the Four Seasons is doing that would make you say to me, 'I love my job'?' Without skipping a beat, Noah said, 'Throughout the day, managers will walk past me and ask me how I'm doing, if there's anything that I need to do my job better.' He said, 'Not my manager, any manager.'

Then he said something magical. He says, 'I also work at Caesars Palace. At Caesars Palace, the managers are trying to make sure we're doing everything right. They catch us when we do things wrong.' He says, 'When I go to work there, I like to keep my head under the radar and get through the day so that I can get my paycheck.' He says, 'Here at the Four Seasons, I feel I can be myself.'

The same person, an entirely different experience for the customer who will engage with Noah. In leadership, we're always criticising the people. We're always saying, 'we got to get the right people on the bus'. I've got to fill my team. I've got to get the right people, but the reality is, it's not the people. It's the leadership. If we create the right environment, we will get people like Noah at the Four Seasons. If we create the wrong environment, we will get people like Noah at Caesars Palace'.

If you treat Noah like he gets treated at Caesars Palace, he may end up leaving in search of another Four Seasons experience.

Noah is in search of a growth-oriented environment. As so often happens in business, we end up keeping the people we don't want to keep, and we lose the people we wish we'd kept.

This means you end up losing an opportunity for growth and innovation and everything else.

The irony is that we often treat our very best people the worst. They end up getting overloaded. Because they take the initiative and have growth mindsets, we view them and treat them differently. We load up extra work on them, and, quite naturally, they get fed up at that after a while and say, 'Why am I running this place for these people with so little appreciation and investment in me?'

Maybe it's you who feels that way: 'Why am I so poorly treated?'

Once someone is unconsciously competent, that means that they've done particularly well with a particular skill. Let's bring this back to an organisational situation now. The thing about it is that competence can exist in almost an infinite number of areas.

Let's take the car example again. We've passed that test; we're unconsciously competent drivers. We're driving around, very relaxed. We don't consciously think about driving, and we quite enjoy it. That means we're only unconsciously competent at driving a car. What about a tank? What about a bus? What about a bicycle? What about an aeroplane? What about a motorboat? What about a Jeep? What about a unicycle?

Just because we can drive one thing doesn't mean we can drive many things. We can be unconsciously competent at driving a car but unconsciously incompetent at driving a motorbike.

Once we get that development journey moving in organisations, where we can consistently develop people, that skill shift from learning how to drive a car to learning how to drive a bike is much smaller because we're in the mode to learn.

Many people say the same about languages. Once you've learnt one extra language, it's much easier to learn a third and a fourth because your brain has worked out that it can elasticate, it can stretch, it can take on board new information. When we've learned how to drive a car, it's much quicker to learn to drive a bike. We still have to go through the four stages, but it is much quicker.

Once we've understood that, we can begin to move into an area that many people call mastery. We're not unconsciously competent at it, but we can master it as a discipline. We become exceptional in that particular area, with that particular skill, with that particular discipline. Again, that's usually through repetition, through ongoing coaching, through leadership. It's important to highlight that coaching is not something that needs to be delivered by someone better than the person. It just needs to be delivered.

Mastery of the Steps

Mastery is that next stage where people can reach a very, very high level of competence. This is the key. This is where we get to the final stage of a learning journey, when the student becomes the teacher. Not to sound like a kung fu movie, but the objective for all training is to turn the trainee into the trainer.

Chapter Four
Why Is Training So Bad?

"An investment in knowledge pays the best interest."
- Benjamin Franklin

The Most Common Training = The Most Common Problem

The most common training is didactic training, which essentially is a lead lecturer delivering information usually from PowerPoint format. That is the most typical training that I see; even online training is often very similar. Content is delivered, and there are questions to be answered. That is it.

This typifies the fundamentally flawed way organisations approach training - viewing it as information to be delivered to people rather than a collaborative process to help the participants get to a higher level of capability. Every time I think about it, it blows my mind - that organisations think that telling people some information somehow correlates with developing their ability to execute brilliantly.

In 1991, Bonwell and Eison described active learning as "anything that involves students doing things and thinking about the things they are doing." But at its core, active learning puts students at the centre and values meaningful creating and collaborating over passively consuming.

Another way to put it. During class time, ask yourself who's working the hardest. If it's you (the lecturer) and not the students, then it might be time to try active learning.

One Simple Change

There are so many ways that training could be improved and made more dynamic, more engaging, and more suitable for different types of learning.

A very simple change that every organisation could make before delivering any training is to ask themselves a simple question, which is: 'What am I trying to achieve by delivering this?' Their answer is frequently wrong - 'we're trying to up-skill them in A, B, C' . What we're trying to do, in reality, is to change behaviour.

All training is aimed at some form of behaviour change. If you think about going to a gym, the aim is not to go to the gym. The aim is to change how you think about your body and health. Training is to change the behaviour. If organisations ask themselves the question, 'Are we going to be able to change their behaviour with this training?' the answer, more often than not, is going to be, 'No.' My advice is very simple. If the training doesn't change behaviour, don't do it.

Just stop wasting money on it. It's better to do no training than to do training poorly, without coaching and mentoring to support it.

Training is so bad because the people delivering it don't have a passion for teaching other people. Often, they haven't reached a level of mastery in that particular subject. Most people who train are competent at what they do.

It's noticeable when you have a master delivering training to you because it feels so different, so intuitive, truly on a different level.

However, it's a rare experience. I'm sure all of us can recall many times where we've had a bad training experience because the person delivering seemed to be disengaged.

Why is training so bad? It's bad because people don't want to make it good. If they did, they would spend three to four times the amount of time they prepare their lesson plans and think about creating the most dynamic, exciting, engaging learning environment. Instead, they focus on, 'Do I have my slides?' They spend most of the time reading from them, occasionally asking the odd perfunctory question to ensure everyone is still awake.

The Usual Attendee Complaints

There are many complaints, and some have been about myself when I've been lazy putting together a particular program. The complaints are consistent.

The first one is usually the most consistent one of all, which is, 'That was boring.'

- 'It went on too long.'
- 'There were too many slides.'

- 'There's too much information; too little interaction.'
- 'I was sat next to the wrong people.'
- 'I didn't learn anything relevant to my job.'
- 'I didn't learn anything that I could do straight away.'
- 'I didn't have anything that I felt was achievable in the long term.'
- 'I didn't have anything that I felt was going to help me do my job better.'
- 'I've heard all of this before.'

The Usual Manager Complaints

- 'Training is a waste of time.'
- 'Training is a waste of money.'
- 'We send them on training days, but they never do anything different.'
- 'I never found out what they covered during the training. I asked them what they covered, and they told me it was fine.'
- 'I didn't know what was going to get covered in the training.'
- 'I haven't seen the feedback forms.'

- 'The training didn't do what I asked it to do.'
- 'The training doesn't directly relate to the jobs.'
- 'The training was too general.'
- 'They didn't ask for my opinion on what should be covered on the training before they were sent on it.'

What Training Should Look Like

Training should be something where, at the end of it, people have self-released a new sense of motivation about what's possible with the subject matter and developed an enthusiasm to implement, as soon as possible, elements of what they learned directly into their work. It should also reinvigorate them around the things that they're already doing well.

Good training is when people identify some of the best practices they're already doing and reinvigorate them and implement them back into their jobs.

Good training should feel like a genuinely exciting experience.

Good training should feel like the trainer is merely facilitating a conversation.

Good training should feel like the exercises are varied and interesting, and challenging.

Good training should feel stressful at times. It should feel difficult at times.

Good training should feel like it was hard work. It should be tiring. It should be challenging.

Good training should feel motivating.

Good training should be varied. There should be defined outputs. There should be clear follow-throughs and plans.

There should be engagement with the leadership on how they can translate what was learned into their roles.

There should be positive and negative feedback. They should be focused on how that training can be improved for next time, to make it better than it was this time. It should identify how this person can be trained and utilise the information. It should also identify how we can accelerate that learning through to mastery so that they can then go and teach other people in the organisation what they've learned and hopefully help them develop and learn new skills as part of that process.

Change Is Active

Change has to be active. If a person has become good at being bad, there will have to be action taken to change that. When we talk about the training being difficult at times, that lets you know, 'Hey, if you want improvement, there has to be change, and for there to be change, there has to be action and movement.'

Essentially, training should take two formats.

It should be a single subject, covered intensively over a one- to three-day period, with follow-on mentoring and coaching optional, or multiple subjects covered over a long period, minimum six months, with consistent and mandatory coaching and mentoring.

Usually, it's the other way around.

It's usually exactly the opposite. It's far too much information trying to be covered in a shorter space of time.

A Quick Story Example

When I was working with a tech pharma company, they had a slide deck. The company made medical equipment. It was an Irish-based company, but its sales team was in the US. The US team would fly over to Ireland, where they were being trained with the existing team.

I was tasked with making sure that they were unconsciously competent within three days. The challenge was we could either spend a great deal of time going through the details of the product, or we could shift the focus to developing a competence around delivering the slide deck, which also had all the medical information in it. If you think about the traditional way people are onboarded, they have to watch a slide deck. They have to take lots of notes, and they have to remember it all, but then they're expected to be already competent, and then they're sent off into the field to do it.

What we did was completely the opposite. We gave them the slide deck, and we said, 'Right, in five minutes, you're going to start delivering that slide deck.' Then, they say, 'Well, I have no script, and I have never delivered it before.' You go, 'Exactly. You're going to start writing your script as you're delivering it.' Then, they say, 'Can we watch someone else do it?' We say, 'No, you're going to do it, and you're going to write your script because it'll be you speaking it.' Then what happens is we give coaching, training, and mentoring, simultaneously and immediately.

Training, Mentoring, & Coaching

You can give them training, and you can give them mentoring and coaching, sometimes seamlessly, sometimes later. You let them run for a while, and then you give it all at once. However, you very intensively pick a single subject like a slide deck. You get them to become masterful at it through massive amounts of training, coaching, and mentoring on one subject delivered over two to three days.

We ran those days from 8:00 am until 5:00 pm until everyone was completely exhausted. By the time they went back to America, the people were unbelievably good at delivering that slide deck, and more importantly, they knew the products inside and out.

My Encouragement to You

It's important not to try to overcommit with your training. It's far better to become masterful in one subject than average in ten. Because training is not a priority, people try to do too much in too little time. The challenge is to pick the top 20%, the highest value things that people could be skilled at, and then focus on delivering that in a very intense, focused way, in a very stressful way, in a very dynamic way, but help them become amazing at it. This will build confidence and enthusiasm for learning about the next thing. My encouragement is to train people in the micro on one subject and take a more macro approach to their overall development by not covering everything in one day.

Chapter Five
Why Should We Mentor?

"Learning should be an active process. Too often, students come to school to watch their teachers work."
- Will Daggett

This next part of the book really speaks to the title of the book: The Lost 90%.

So much of what is wrong is wrapped up in this missing piece. There is almost universal agreement that mentoring and coaching on the job should make up 90% of any person's learning and development journey. It should be supported by the organisation, with leaders and managers fully engaged and everyone else feeling a real investment in their growth. Finding 'The Lost 90%' is the fastest way to grow your organisation, regardless of its focus.

It gives people disproportionate leverage.

It gives people the chance to be part of an organisation that really makes a difference.

It gives people the chance to take off.

It helps people get closer to fulfilling their potential and the potential of the people that surround them.

It is time to stop wasting money on just training and address the elephant in the room. You need The Lost 90% put back into your organisation and not just on the sidelines. At the centre of everything you do. If we invest in growth, we get growth. Developing confidence and competence is the only logical way to do it.

This is a change of behaviour. I hope the change can start now as you read the rest of this book.

"Learning is "something an individual does when he studies. It is an active, personally conducted affair." - John Dewey - Democracy and Education (1924)

Why Should We Mentor?

Most people don't mentor their employees because one of the most important elements of mentoring is giving feedback, and most people feel strangely awkward giving feedback to people about anything. Most of us prefer not to tell people what they're doing wrong - it feels uncomfortable, and we are naturally conflict-averse - nor do we want to hurt people's feelings or damage their self-esteem. So we shy away from being truthful and direct. Look at the classic restaurant situation where you've had a bad dinner. The waiter comes over and says, 'How was your meal?', to which most people invariably answer: 'It was fine, thank you.' Then, as soon as you're ready to leave, you go, 'This is the worst restaurant in the world. We're never coming here again.' Because we don't like to give feedback.

We Don't Like to Tell People What's Wrong

We don't even know how to give feedback. The role of mentoring is to develop competence and confidence, and to do that, we must be honest with people, but managers struggle to be honest too.

Why do so few people mentor their employees? There's a requirement to be honest. There's a requirement to be direct. There's a requirement to receive feedback too, which is also equally uncomfortable for many people, especially those in a leadership or management position. They don't want to receive feedback. They want to be told they're doing a great job, and it's extremely uncomfortable for an employee to tell a manager the way they've explained something isn't accurate or good enough to help them develop.

But managers are also not properly engaged with the development of their employees. They view it as a big time thief, so they don't think it's worth putting the time and effort in because they've had some bad experiences with some previous employees or maybe some current ones. It kills the motivation to do it. They allow the good people to be good people, and they allow the poor people to be poor people, which encourages the good people to leave and encourages the poor people to stay.

Overcoming Myths & Misunderstandings

The main myth about mentoring is that it's the same as coaching. They are two words that are often used interchangeably, but they're actually fundamentally different.

Mentoring is a collaborative relationship. It needs both parties to speak openly and directly to each other and undertake a combination of showing how something should be done, sharing that task or skill or development opportunity. Then the learner needs to show competence, to show that they've understood and that they can do it, to show that they've reached stage three of the learning journey, which is conscious competence.

The role of mentoring is to get the person to conscious competence. It's not to help them become unconsciously competent. It's not to make them masterful. It's not to help them teach. It's to make sure that they feel competent in the execution of any particular task.

The major myth or misunderstanding is what the role of mentoring is. I think it's often misunderstood as coaching. People often think that when they're mentoring, they're coaching and vice versa. It's quite clear that mentoring is fundamentally not like coaching. On the foundational basis, to mentor effectively, you need to have an opinion.

In coaching, it's fundamentally important that you don't revert to the training thing again. The snake has eaten itself. They're shouting at them, arbitrarily telling them what to do.

A good example of where mentoring really matters is that employee who is either in the middle of an onboarding process or has had very little development in the past. Let's say they're in that 'No Man's Land' of two to five years when many people switch jobs or look for a promotion. I think mentoring at that point can be vital - it's where you identify what their future skills should be, reiterate the organisational strategy and demonstrate how learning fresh skills can help the individual and the business to grow.

Mentoring can help introduce them to other people in the organisation and consolidate their position there. Mentoring can help keep people in a role and save recruitment costs because they feel the investment, engagement, and value shown in their time.

Mentoring Is Key

For me, mentoring is such a key part because it revolves around steps two and three of the learning journey. At the stage of conscious incompetence, when we recognise that we need to develop in multiple areas, mentoring can help to build confidence and competence.

When we reach stage three, conscious competence, the mentor can help consolidate that skill and identify the next step - 'Okay, great; you've become amazing at handling transactions on the tail. What other areas of our business could you learn about and transfer some of those skills to?'

The mentor's job is to maintain that vibe of learning and development, and growth. Mentoring can save the day. It can completely and profoundly change an organisation if it's done consistently.

Avoid tokenism

The danger with mentoring is that it can become tokenistic. Say the buddy leaves, or the support person leaves, or you go through a busy period in the operation where there's a product launch, a change in management, or a new strategy that needs to be delivered. At those times frequently, the mentor stops mentoring simply because they're busy. The danger is when the shift goes from learning and goes back to tasks.

What Proper Mentoring Looks Like

As discussed, mentoring usually involves some demonstration of competence. For the mentor to show what good looks like usually involves sharing that task and deploying a collaborative approach to any new skill being developed, where the mentor and the mentee are jointly involved in the learning and development.

It's not about telling them what to do but instead actively engaging in developing competence. For example, the mentor might start a particular task, but then the mentee might complete it. For the next version, the mentee might start, and then the mentor might finish. That collaboration demonstrates the value of the investment and also has the benefit of allowing the mentee to show their demonstration of competence.

This is how it should work - showing them, sharing it with them, and getting them to show you. The way it's delivered is through consistent feedback. For the mentor and the mentee, it's a living, dynamic relationship. Opinions and ideas are welcomed - fresh thinking and fresh thoughts from both parties. This is a positive upward trajectory towards the development of competence both as a mentor and from the mentee's point of view, learning a new skill. In a good mentoring situation, the mentor should be learning as much as the mentee.

Chapter Six
The Power of a Great Coach

" Education is not an affair of 'telling' and being told, but an active and constructive process. "
- John Dewey

The main reason so many companies overlook the power of coaching is that they don't understand what coaching is. Most organisations understand what mentoring is, but they aren't necessarily well disposed towards it because of the reasons mentioned around honesty and feedback. But many organisations don't truly know what coaching is - perhaps they're anecdotally aware of sports coaching, but they don't really know how to execute coaching professionally in their own organisation.

The most consistent thing I've observed is the gap between the perception of how good managers think they are at coaching and their actual ability to coach. People think they're good coaches, but what they've been quite good at is just telling people what to do, whilst believing they are being helpful and coaching their team.

They think they've been helpful because they've been giving definitive answers, but what they've been doing is limiting their people's development and growth. It's quicker to tell someone what to do than to coach them on it, and because it's quicker to tell them what to do, that's usually the default position. In many ways, that's what training is.

Training is giving someone new skills or knowledge that they should start to learn to implement.

Mentoring is developing confidence and competence in how to implement those skills.

Coaching is not about skill acquisition. They have the skill. Coaching is when it's behavioural. Coaching is when your opinion is no longer relevant, and it's there as a facilitative function to get people to realise that potential.

Two Rules of Coaching

There are two fundamental rules of coaching.

Rule #1

Rule number one is that a good coach knows nothing. That doesn't mean that you know nothing, of course. It means that your opinion is not required because, when we offer our opinion, we're usually solving the problem in front of us with our answer, and often, our answer is not the most up-to-date or relevant. That's not the point. It is not the coach's problem to decode - the issue that they're addressing is usually not their problem. If they try and solve the problem for the person through suggestions and actions, the mentee is not really benefiting. It is not about sector expertise on the coach's behalf; it's about effective questioning and accountability.

Rule #2

Rule number two is that everyone has the potential to do more. This doesn't mean they will fulfil that potential, but that in itself is not the coach's problem. The coach is only there to bring accountability to that potential.

If someone doesn't fulfil that potential, then through effective questioning, we need to challenge why they're engaged with a coach. If they are fulfilling their potential, the coach's role is to help them find a new level of performance that they previously hadn't reached. We mentioned it already, but all of the world's top athletes have coaches. This is not because the coach is better than the athlete. It's because coaches challenge behaviour.

Changing Perceptions

Some organisations simply think they don't need a coaching culture. Others may not have ever even considered using coaching. At least the first situation is one where they've considered coaching and rejected it. The second situation is where they have not tried to understand what the potential value can be. Again, if we go back to chapter one in the book of teaching versus learning, this often reveals a pretty basic lack of understanding of how a high level of performance is reached. Time and time again, it's been proven that financial incentives don't deliver consistently better performance. All they do is require a higher level of incentive to deliver a higher level of performance. That's not intrinsically motivating to people.

It's a massive issue for organisations that they don't get people to perform to a high level. It's like they see humans as non-exceptional, whereas athletes and artists, well, they're special because they've got talent. It goes back to that fixed mindset thing. There's a view from organisations that there are talented people, then there are untalented people, whereas coaching posits that everyone has the potential to do more.

It's a fundamentally different way of thinking about your human resource. You think about, 'How can I develop my people to achieve the results we want?' But as we've mentioned, organisations are more often focused on 'What tasks do we need to do to be successful?'

The Evolution of Coaching

The evolution of sports coaches is interesting. Have you noticed how many coaches on the sidelines don't jump up and down or shout orders? They sit there calmly and watch the game. At that point, they've recognised there's very little they can do apart from being tuned into the tactics and the strategy. It's not about them.

In a learning environment, discussion is one of the most common strategies promoting active learning.

Research has suggested that to achieve these goals, the faculty must be knowledgeable of alternative techniques and strategies for questioning and discussion (Hyman 1980) and must create a supportive intellectual and emotional environment that encourages students to take risks (Lowman 1984).

Chapter Seven
Training, Mentoring, and Coaching Mistakes to Avoid

"The delicate balance of mentoring someone is not creating them in your own image, but giving them the opportunity to create themselves."
- Steven Spielberg

What might be good here is to define, formally, what training is, what mentoring is and what coaching is.

- Training is teaching someone a skill they don't currently have.
- Mentoring is developing their confidence and competence in that skill.
- Coaching develops the behaviours around that skill to support that person's long-term growth, ultimately leading to them becoming masterful and a teacher in that particular subject.

Training Mistake

One mistake people make in training is a fundamental one - they don't know what they're trying to get out of it. The key issue or challenge is that they shouldn't try and do training if it doesn't change behaviour. The training needs to try and change behaviour fundamentally.

Mentoring Mistake

The key mistake in mentoring is being afraid of what people might have to say and what you might have to say. Adults like feedback when it's delivered well.

Coaching Mistake

The coaching mistake is thinking that the problem of the person you're coaching is your problem. It's not your job to fix their problem. It's to help them fix their own and achieve their fullest potential.

A Homework Assignment for You

Do a self-assessment. If we go back to the difference between learning and teaching, I would ask you to reflect on the different types of organisation I described earlier, determine which one you fit most closely with, and think about how happy you are with that.

There was a type where there's no investment in training, mentoring, or coaching. It's 'do your job', top-down, low morale, task-focused.

There was the reactive type - offering training, mentoring, and coaching based on external factors. There was no personal development plan. There's only a focus on the business needs, and they're usually used to correct performance or deliver something mandatory.

The process is usually driven by HR. It's standardised, off-the-shelf. It's usually in-house. It's a box-ticking exercise, a necessary evil. They're appraised annually, and there are minimal amounts of mentoring and coaching involved.

Then the final type is development, where learning is the main priority, not tasks.

Accountability, ownership, and responsibility are important throughout the organisation. It's a 'leaders and learners' culture. Training focuses on turning that trainee into the trainer, into the teacher, growth-oriented, collaborative, team-oriented, and positive.

Freeman's 2014 paper presents a meta-analysis of 225 studies reporting either exam scores or failure rates related to traditional lecture vs. active learning in undergraduate STEM courses. A general summary of findings is that average exam scores improve by around 6% in active learning classes, and students taking courses with traditional lectures are 1.5 times more likely to fail than those in classes with active learning.

My Encouragement to You

There's no reason not to change the organisational culture to learning and development, when results can rapidly have a positive impact. In terms of a transformation, there's very little else you can do so cost-effectively that can deliver such a disproportionate result for your organisation.

Fundamentally, it's changing the words you use and changing your attitudes towards the people you have working for you. In most cases, your people are your most expensive resource and should be treated accordingly, yet often, they get treated as the most inconvenient and are only valued by their results. Investing in people will deliver immediate and very positive results. That is a fact.

Finding Your Lost 90%

The Lost 90% can be found. You'll recognise that the joy, the fun, the happiness of being in an organisation and working with people is that the work should always be secondary and the people should always be primary. Work can be positive, engaging, dynamic, and enjoyable if that's the focus.

If the focus is on tasks, then work can only become stressful, demoralising, and demotivating and will ultimately end in people leaving the organisation or their mental or physical health suffering. Investing in people is the most positive thing you can do, no more than investing in yourself.

When you implement The Lost 90%, the transformation can happen within weeks. The transformation can happen within 24 or 48 hours in some cases. Unlike nearly any other thing you can do, when you shift to bringing in The Lost 90% of mentoring and coaching, you put some effort into thinking about how training might be dynamic, fun, exciting, positive, useful, and transformative, and result in behavioural change. The translation in terms of your results can be delivered within weeks.

I worked with an organisation in Belgium, a pharmaceutical company missing their target for two and a half years. We brought a coaching culture and skill set to their field leadership team, and within eight weeks, they hit their budget after two and a half years spent missing it. That was sustained for at least 18 months after that. All we did was upskill six people on how to coach, mentor and lead their teams. It took eight weeks to transform the company from missing budget to hitting budget.

For more information, please read one of our other books to help understand learning cultures and how you can make changes straight away and develop a learning culture that you can be proud of and proud to work in. For more information, visit my website, which is **www.yourlearninglegacy.com**

How to Stop Wasting Money on Training & Grow Exponentially

You've done a great job recruiting employees and training them for their new positions. You have manuals, meetings, and hours of seminars for their onboarding process. Wouldn't it be fantastic if those onboarding sessions could be properly engaging? Can you imagine what potential you could see evolve if your employees were excited to participate in the training?

We all have the potential to do more. When people are freed from functional thinking and are able to be creative, committed, and engaged, they deliver disproportionate value. But they must be engaged with the mentors and coaches. That's why 'The Lost 90%' program was developed. We help organisations like yours regain the potential for growth through proper training, mentoring, and coaching.

To learn more about the ideas discussed in this book, here's what you do next.

Step 1:

Take the business diagnostic to understand what type of organisation you are at **www.yourlearninglegacy.com/business-diagnostic**

Step 2:

Arrange a call with me using this link to my calendar **calendly.com/robmarr/the-lost-90**

Step 3:

Start to make some small changes outlined in the book. It could just be a simple step like asking what your team thinks of how they are being developed and what their suggestions might be to kickstart it!

The Last Word

I hope you treat this as a call to action! Your people are your greatest resource, and they need investment, just like any piece of infrastructure in your organisation.

You should view this as mandatory - you should be thinking about the potential for growth by putting people at the centre of your growth plans. Not just as a functional part.

You should boost your investment by 90%, and I don't just mean training. I mean, on the time it takes to genuinely and completely invest and commit to your people.

As a trainer, I can confidently say that training doesn't work on its own, and anyone selling you just training isn't aligned to your growth. They are selling you something that is inherently designed to fail. There is a Lost 90% in our development journey, and until you find it, you will keep wasting money, seeing very little return on your investment.

Put simply…

<u>If it doesn't or won't or can't change behaviour, then don't do it</u>

It is time to find your LOST 90%

Made in the USA
Middletown, DE
26 April 2022

64736488R00057